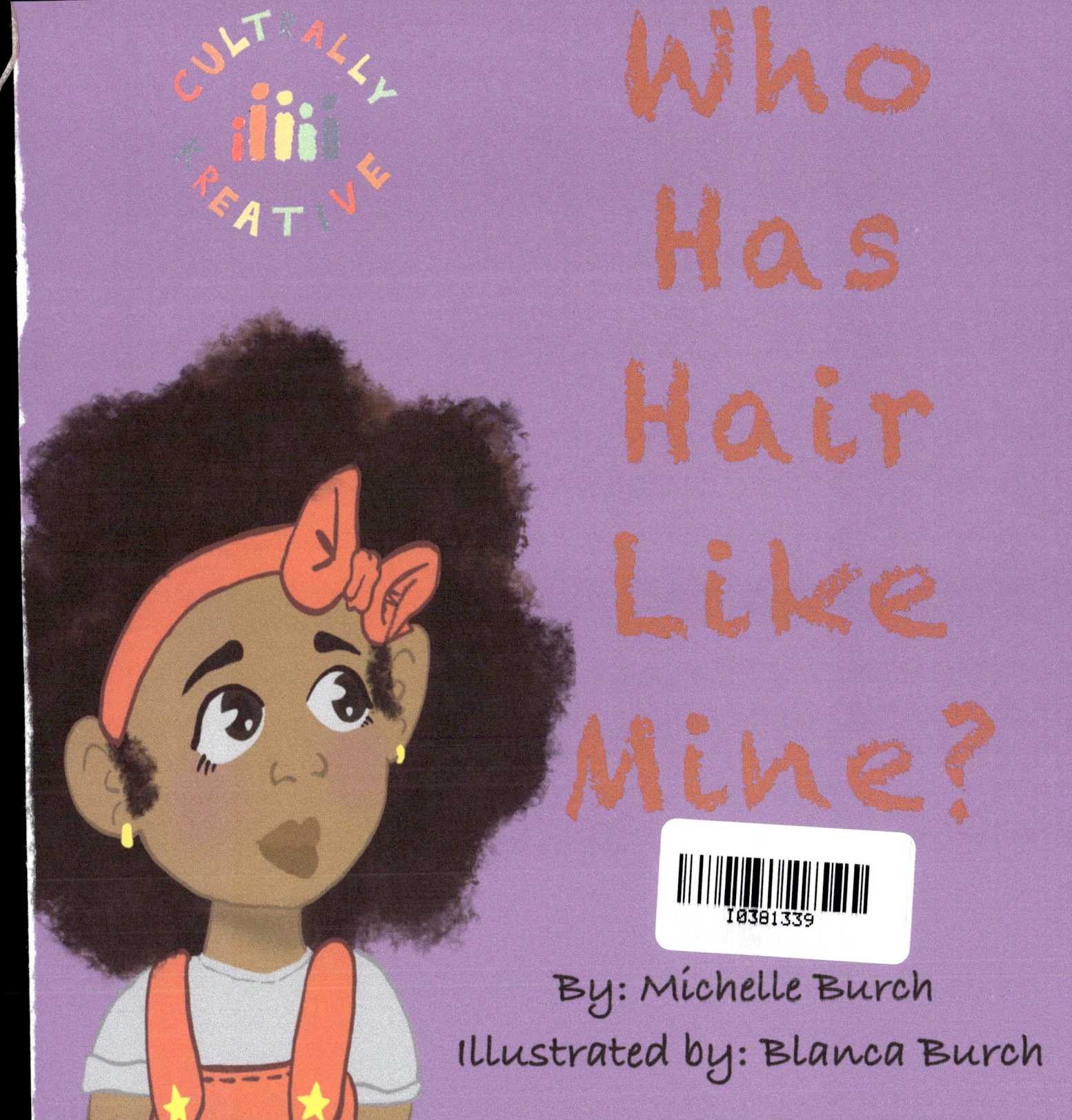

Copyright © 2020 by Blanca Burch and Michelle Burch

All rights reserved. Published in the United States by Culturally Kreative. No part of this publication may be reproduced, distributed, or transmitted in any form or by any means, including photocopying, recording, or other electronic or mechanical methods, without the prior written permission of the publisher, except in the case of brief quotations embodied in critical reviews and certain other noncommercial uses permitted by copyright law. For permission requests, write to the publisher, addressed "Attention: Permissions Coordinator," at:Culturally Kreative
129 Lamplighter Lane Racine, WI 53402

Visit us on the Web! www.culturallykreative.com

Educators and librarians, for a variety of teaching tools, visit us at Culturallykreative.com

Library of Congress Cataloging-in- Publication Data: Burch, Blanca, Burch, Michelle

Who Has Hair Like Mine? / by Michelle Burch ; Illustrated by Blanca Burch

P. cm.

ISBN 978-1-7352218-0-9 (paperback) | ISBN 978-1-7352218-1-6 (ebook) |

ISBN 978-1-7352218-2-3 (Hardcover)

Subjects: | Hair-Fiction |Hairstyles-Fiction | African-Americans-Fiction |

Self-esteem- Fiction.

Ordering Information:

Quantity sales. Special discounts are available on quantity purchases by corporations, associations, and others. For details, contact the publisher at the address above.

Orders by U.S. trade bookstores and wholesalers. www.culturallykreative.com

Printed in the United States of America

Why does my hair look different from the girls in this magazine?

4

Do you see Serenity? Her hair is straightened. To get that look, I would typically wash and blow dry the hair. Next, I apply direct heat to the hair with a flat iron. This process will smooth out her hair's natural curl pattern.

12

Look over there. Do you see Thomas? He has a tight curl pattern and wears a tapered cut. His hair is longer at the top, and it gradually gets shorter down the back and sides of his head.

Look at Lauren and Elijah. Lauren likes to style her own hair. Elijah has a short cut. Stylists use clippers to "line him up". He goes to a barber every week to maintain that style.

Well it depends.
I think you just need to try out different styles and find out what works best for your hair.

There's Christy! She has relaxed hair. A relaxer is a chemical treatment that straigtens the hair. It is reapplied every six to eight weeks. In my opinion, it makes hair easier to manage.

Mom, what else can you do to hair?

I also color hair. My clients add color to change their look, or even to cover gray hair. Grace, Genesis, and Kennedy are scheduled for color later today. I will apply a chemical to their hair and it will change the color of their hair.

Those are extensions. Clients choose what they like and I style it. Today, Nisa and Lani are using hair extensions to get braids before they go on vacation.

Braids can be...

Thin

Long

Hair extensions come in a variety of styles, textures, and colors. I can braid clients or bond extensions to their hair. Look around. These four pictures are some of my clients with their extensions washed and curled.

31

What style will you give Sophie?

37

About the Illustrator

Blanca Burch was born and raised in Milwaukee, Wisconsin. She is an entrepreneur and a self-taught graphic designer. She is also co-founder of Culturally Kreative. Currently, Blanca is an International Studies major and Management and Organization minor at Spelman College. Outside of school she works with youth in her community.

About the Author

Born and raised in Milwaukee, Wisconsin, Michelle Burch is an entrepreneur, educator, and reading specialist with over two decades of teaching experience. She is co-founder of Culturally Kreative. She currently is an Instructional Methods Coordiator for the Racine Unified School District where she empowers, encourages, and positively impacts teachers and students.

www.ingramcontent.com/pod-product-compliance
Lightning Source LLC
Chambersburg PA
CBHW042029100526
44587CB00029B/4352